MAD LIBS

MAD ABOUT ANIMALS MAD LIBS

By Roger Price and Leonard Stern

PSS!
PRICE STERN SLOAN

PRICE STERN SLOAN
Published by the Penguin Group
Penguin Group (USA) Inc., 375 Hudson Street, New York, New York 10014, USA
Penguin Group (Canada), 90 Eglinton Avenue East, Suite 700,
Toronto, Ontario M4P 2Y3, Canada
(a division of Pearson Penguin Canada Inc.)
Penguin Books Ltd., 80 Strand, London WC2R 0RL, England
Penguin Group Ireland, 25 St. Stephen's Green, Dublin 2, Ireland
(a division of Penguin Books Ltd.)
Penguin Group (Australia), 250 Camberwell Road, Camberwell, Victoria 3124, Australia
(a division of Pearson Australia Group Pty. Ltd.)
Penguin Books India Pvt. Ltd., 11 Community Centre,
Panchsheel Park, New Delhi—110 017, India
Penguin Group (NZ), 67 Apollo Drive, Rosedale, North Shore 0632, New Zealand
(a division of Pearson New Zealand Ltd.)
Penguin Books (South Africa) (Pty.) Ltd., 24 Sturdee Avenue,
Rosebank, Johannesburg 2196, South Africa

Penguin Books Ltd., Registered Offices:
80 Strand, London WC2R 0RL, England

Published by Price Stern Sloan,
a division of Penguin Young Readers Group,
345 Hudson Street, New York, New York 10014.

ISBN 978-0-8431-3713-2

19 18 17

MAD LIBS®
INSTRUCTIONS

MAD LIBS® is a game for people who don't like games!
It can be played by one, two, three, four, or forty.

• RIDICULOUSLY SIMPLE DIRECTIONS

In this tablet you will find stories containing blank spaces where words
are left out. One player, the READER, selects one of these stories. The
READER does not tell anyone what the story is about. Instead, he/she asks
the other players, the WRITERS, to give him/her words. These words are
used to fill in the blank spaces in the story.

• TO PLAY

The READER asks each WRITER in turn to call out a word—an adjective or
a noun or whatever the space calls for—and uses them to fill in the blank
spaces in the story. The result is a MAD LIBS® game.

When the READER then reads the completed MAD LIBS® game to the other
players, they will discover that they have written a story that is fantastic,
screamingly funny, shocking, silly, crazy, or just plain dumb—depending
upon which words each WRITER called out.

• EXAMPLE (*Before* and *After*)

"_____!" he said _____
      EXCLAMATION   ADVERB

as he jumped into his convertible _____ and
                NOUN

drove off with his _____ wife.
         ADJECTIVE

"*Ouch*!" he said *Stupidly*
      EXCLAMATION   ADVERB

as he jumped into his convertible *cat* and
                NOUN

drove off with his *brave* wife.
         ADJECTIVE

In case you have forgotten what adjectives, adverbs, nouns, and verbs are, here is a quick review:

An ADJECTIVE describes something or somebody. *Lumpy*, *soft*, *ugly*, *messy*, and *short* are adjectives.

An ADVERB tells how something is done. It modifies a verb and usually ends in "ly." *Modestly*, *stupidly*, *greedily*, and *carefully* are adverbs.

A NOUN is the name of a person, place, or thing. *Sidewalk*, *umbrella*, *bridle*, *bathtub*, and *nose* are nouns.

A VERB is an action word. *Run*, *pitch*, *jump*, and *swim* are verbs. Put the verbs in past tense if the directions say PAST TENSE. *Ran*, *pitched*, *jumped*, and *swam* are verbs in the past tense.

When we ask for A PLACE, we mean any sort of place: a country or city (*Spain*, *Cleveland*) or a room (*bathroom*, *kitchen*).

An EXCLAMATION or SILLY WORD is any sort of funny sound, gasp, grunt, or outcry, like *Wow!*, *Ouch!*, *Whomp!*, *Ick!*, and *Gadzooks!*

When we ask for specific words, like a NUMBER, a COLOR, an ANIMAL, or a PART OF THE BODY, we mean a word that is one of those things, like *seven*, *blue*, *horse*, or *head*.

When we ask for a PLURAL, it means more than one. For example, *cat* pluralized is *cats*.

MAD LIBS® is fun to play with friends, but you can also play it by yourself! To begin with, DO NOT look at the story on the page below. Fill in the blanks on this page with the words called for. Then, using the words you have selected, fill in the blank spaces in the story.

Now you've created your own hilarious MAD LIBS® game!

DOG'S POINT OF VIEW

PERSON IN ROOM (MALE) _____

PART OF THE BODY (PLURAL) _____

NOUN _____

PART OF THE BODY _____

ADJECTIVE _____

ADVERB _____

NOUN _____

ADJECTIVE _____

ADJECTIVE _____

PART OF THE BODY _____

PART OF THE BODY (PLURAL) _____

ADJECTIVE _____

PLURAL NOUN _____

PLURAL NOUN _____

VERB _____

ADJECTIVE _____

NOUN _____

ADJECTIVE _____

NOUN _____

MAD LIBS®
DOG'S POINT OF VIEW

The minute I saw _____ pucker his _____
PERSON IN ROOM (MALE)   PART OF THE BODY (PLURAL)

and whistle, I knew we were going for a/an _____
NOUN

ride. I wagged my _____, gave a/an _____
PART OF THE BODY   ADJECTIVE

bark, and _____ leaped into the back- _____
ADVERB   NOUN

of the car. As we began our _____ drive through the
ADJECTIVE

_____ neighborhood, I stuck my _____
ADJECTIVE   PART OF THE BODY

out the window, felt the wind in my _____,
PART OF THE BODY (PLURAL)

and took in all the _____ smells. We drove past cars,
ADJECTIVE

people, and _____. Then it hit me like a ton of
PLURAL NOUN

_____—we were headed for the dog park! I'd get to
PLURAL NOUN

see and _____ with my _____ girlfriend,
VERB   ADJECTIVE

Fifi, who is a purebred French _____. Yes, sir, despite
NOUN

all the _____ publicity, there's nothing like a dog's life
ADJECTIVE

when you have a generous and caring _____ like mine.
NOUN

MAD LIBS® is fun to play with friends, but you can also play it by yourself! To begin with, DO NOT look at the story on the page below. Fill in the blanks on this page with the words called for. Then, using the words you have selected, fill in the blank spaces in the story.

Now you've created your own hilarious MAD LIBS® game!

POSTCARD FROM A SAFARI

ADJECTIVE _____

ADJECTIVE _____

PLURAL NOUN _____

NOUN _____

PLURAL NOUN _____

TYPE OF LIQUID _____

ADJECTIVE _____

A PLACE _____

NOUN _____

NOUN _____

NOUN _____

PART OF THE BODY _____

ADJECTIVE _____

ADJECTIVE _____

NUMBER _____

NOUN _____

VERB ENDING IN "ING" _____

MAD LIBS®

POSTCARD FROM A SAFARI

Wish you were here on this _____ African safari!
                              ADJECTIVE

We are having the most _____ time of our
                            ADJECTIVE

_____. Believe it or not, on the first day, we saw a
   PLURAL NOUN

mother _____ and her baby _____
              NOUN   PLURAL NOUN

drinking _____ from a watering hole. The second
            TYPE OF LIQUID

day, we climbed onto the back of a/an _____
                                          ADJECTIVE

elephant and went through (the) _____, and the
                                      A PLACE

beauty took my _____ away. But the best—and
                     NOUN

weirdest—part was saved for last. We were deep in the forest

when a huge _____ climbed onto the hood of our
                   NOUN

_____ and took a swipe at us with its powerful
      NOUN

_____. But as this letter attests, we survived. All in
   PART OF THE BODY

all, this has been a really _____ trip. Thankfully you'll
                                ADJECTIVE

be able to share our _____ adventures because I've
                          ADJECTIVE

taken more than _____ pictures with my trusty digital
                      NUMBER

_____. As they say, seeing is _____!
   NOUN   VERB ENDING IN "ING"

From MAD ABOUT ANIMALS MAD LIBS® • Copyright © 2009 by Price Stern Sloan,
a division of Penguin Young Readers Group, 345 Hudson Street, New York, NY 10014.

MAD LIBS® is fun to play with friends, but you can also play it by yourself! To begin with, DO NOT look at the story on the page below. Fill in the blanks on this page with the words called for. Then, using the words you have selected, fill in the blank spaces in the story.

Now you've created your own hilarious MAD LIBS® game!

AUSTRALIAN WILDLIFE

NOUN _____

ADJECTIVE _____

NOUN _____

PART OF THE BODY (PLURAL) _____

NOUN _____

ADJECTIVE _____

PLURAL NOUN _____

PLURAL NOUN _____

PLURAL NOUN _____

NOUN _____

PLURAL NOUN _____

NOUN _____

NOUN _____

PLURAL NOUN _____

ADJECTIVE _____

MAD LIBS®

AUSTRALIAN WILDLIFE

Australia, also known as the _____ Down Under,

NOUN

is famous for its _____ wildlife. The most

ADJECTIVE

famous animal is the kangaroo, which carries its baby in a/an

_____ on its belly and travels by hopping on its

NOUN

powerful hind _____. The koala is another popular

PART OF THE BODY (PLURAL)

Australian _____. This furry, _____

NOUN ADJECTIVE

creature loves to eat leaves from eucalyptus _____. If

PLURAL NOUN

you are a bird-watcher, the emu will knock your _____

PLURAL NOUN

off. It is a bird that has no _____ and cannot fly, but

PLURAL NOUN

it can run faster than a speeding _____. Perhaps the

NOUN

strangest of all Australian _____ is the platypus. It has a

PLURAL NOUN

bill that resembles a duck's _____ and the body of

NOUN

a/an _____. It is one of only two mammals that lay

NOUN

_____ instead of giving birth to their young. If you

PLURAL NOUN

are a nature lover, you must put exotic and _____

ADJECTIVE

Australia on your places-to-go list!

From MAD ABOUT ANIMALS MAD LIBS® • Copyright © 2009 by Price Stern Sloan,
a division of Penguin Young Readers Group, 345 Hudson Street, New York, NY 10014.

MAD LIBS® is fun to play with friends, but you can also play it by yourself! To begin with, DO NOT look at the story on the page below. Fill in the blanks on this page with the words called for. Then, using the words you have selected, fill in the blank spaces in the story.

Now you've created your own hilarious MAD LIBS® game!

SCHOOL PET FRET

ADJECTIVE _____

PERSON IN ROOM (MALE) _____

ADJECTIVE _____

NOUN _____

NOUN _____

NOUN _____

PART OF THE BODY _____

VERB ENDING IN "ING" _____

ADVERB _____

NUMBER _____

PLURAL NOUN _____

ADJECTIVE _____

ADJECTIVE _____

ADJECTIVE _____

EXCLAMATION _____

PLURAL NOUN _____

MAD LIBS®

SCHOOL PET FRET

I recently had the honor of taking our class pet, a/an _____
                                                              ADJECTIVE

rabbit named _____, to my house for the weekend.
              PERSON IN ROOM (MALE)

I carried the little guy in his _____ cage and left him
                                 ADJECTIVE

on the kitchen _____ as I went about my afternoon
                 NOUN

chores of unloading the _____-washer and taking out the
                          NOUN

_____. When I came back, my _____ dropped
 NOUN   PART OF THE BODY

open in shock. He was gone! My heart was _____ a mile
                                           VERB ENDING IN "ING"

a minute as I _____ ran through the house. I checked
               ADVERB

every room at least _____ times. Desperate, I even checked
                     NUMBER

my pile of dirty _____ twice. But I couldn't find him
                  PLURAL NOUN

anywhere. Finally I heard a/an _____ noise and I followed
                                ADJECTIVE

it to the basement. There, right next to the _____
                                              ADJECTIVE

water heater, was my classroom's precious rabbit—with five

_____ baby rabbits. _____! The *he* was a *she*!
 ADJECTIVE   EXCLAMATION

And she had just given birth to a litter of _____!
                                             PLURAL NOUN

From MAD ABOUT ANIMALS MAD LIBS® • Copyright © 2009 by Price Stern Sloan,
a division of Penguin Young Readers Group, 345 Hudson Street, New York, NY 10014.

MAD LIBS® is fun to play with friends, but you can also play it by yourself! To begin with, DO NOT look at the story on the page below. Fill in the blanks on this page with the words called for. Then, using the words you have selected, fill in the blank spaces in the story.

Now you've created your own hilarious MAD LIBS® game!

CALLING ALL BIRDS

ADJECTIVE _____

NOUN _____

ADJECTIVE _____

ADJECTIVE _____

NOUN _____

ADJECTIVE _____

PART OF THE BODY _____

NOUN _____

ADJECTIVE _____

PART OF THE BODY _____

NOUN _____

ADJECTIVE _____

NOUN _____

NOUN _____

NOUN _____

MAD LIBS®

CALLING ALL BIRDS

Every bird has a/an _____ song or call—and every

ADJECTIVE

talented _____-watcher knows how to imitate them

NOUN

precisely. The following three _____ birds can be easily

ADJECTIVE

imitated by a/an _____ amateur.

ADJECTIVE

• The yellow-bellied sap _____: A/An _____

NOUN ADJECTIVE

   member of the woodpecker family, its call can be easily

   reproduced by squeezing your _____ as tightly as

PART OF THE BODY

   possible and meowing like a hungry _____.

NOUN

• The pelican: Its _____ call is easy to repeat, provided

ADJECTIVE

   you stretch your _____ to its fullest length before

PART OF THE BODY

   emitting a squawk-like _____.

NOUN

• The cockatoo: Its vocalization is loud and _____.

ADJECTIVE

   But cockatoos primarily emit a soft, growling _____

NOUN

   when feeding. They also communicate by drumming a dead

   _____ with a stick. And when threatened, they issue

NOUN

   an easily duplicated hissing _____.

NOUN

MAD LIBS® is fun to play with friends, but you can also play it by yourself! To begin with, DO NOT look at the story on the page below. Fill in the blanks on this page with the words called for. Then, using the words you have selected, fill in the blank spaces in the story.

Now you've created your own hilarious MAD LIBS® game!

FIELD TRIP TO THE ZOO

ADJECTIVE _____

ADJECTIVE _____

ADJECTIVE _____

ADJECTIVE _____

ADJECTIVE _____

PLURAL NOUN _____

PLURAL NOUN _____

ADJECTIVE _____

PART OF THE BODY (PLURAL) _____

NOUN _____

ADJECTIVE _____

PLURAL NOUN _____

PLURAL NOUN _____

ADJECTIVE _____

NOUN _____

PART OF THE BODY (PLURAL) _____

PERSON IN ROOM _____

PART OF THE BODY _____

MAD☉LIBS®
FIELD TRIP TO THE ZOO

Okay, class! Here we are at the _____ zoo. It is a/an
                                    ADJECTIVE

_____ place to enjoy _____ experiences,
ADJECTIVE   ADJECTIVE

but in order to do so, you must obey these _____ rules.
                                              ADJECTIVE

Rule #1 is personal: Have a/an _____ time.
                                  ADJECTIVE

Rule #2: Please don't feed the _____. They eat
                                  PLURAL NOUN

scientifically formulated _____ to ensure they
                             PLURAL NOUN

remain in _____ health. Human food can upset
             ADJECTIVE

their _____ and make them sicker than a/an
         PART OF THE BODY (PLURAL)

_____.
NOUN

Rule #3: Don't litter. Make sure you throw all of your _____
                                                          ADJECTIVE

wrappers and plastic _____ into trash _____
                        PLURAL NOUN   PLURAL NOUN

to keep the zoo sparkling and _____.
                                 ADJECTIVE

Rule #4: Respect boundaries. When you approach a wild _____
                                                         NOUN

cage, keep your _____ to yourself at all times. Last
                   PART OF THE BODY (PLURAL)

year, _____ attempted to pet an orangutan and almost
         PERSON IN ROOM

lost his/her left _____.
                     PART OF THE BODY

MAD LIBS® is fun to play with friends, but you can also play it by yourself! To begin with, DO NOT look at the story on the page below. Fill in the blanks on this page with the words called for. Then, using the words you have selected, fill in the blank spaces in the story.

Now you've created your own hilarious MAD LIBS® game!

LEGENDARY CREATURES

ADJECTIVE _____

ADJECTIVE _____

PLURAL NOUN _____

NOUN _____

ADJECTIVE _____

PLURAL NOUN _____

A PLACE _____

ADJECTIVE _____

NOUN _____

PART OF THE BODY _____

NOUN _____

ADJECTIVE _____

ADJECTIVE _____

NOUN _____

PLURAL NOUN _____

PLURAL NOUN _____

ADJECTIVE _____

MAD☉LIBS®

LEGENDARY CREATURES

Throughout time, man has heard _____ tales of
ADJECTIVE

_____, mythical creatures that challenge the imagination.
ADJECTIVE

Here are the most famous of these _____:
PLURAL NOUN

• The **mermaid**, half human, half _____, was known to
NOUN

sing _____ songs that caused sailors to crash their
ADJECTIVE

_____ in the middle of (the) _____.
PLURAL NOUN   A PLACE

• The **unicorn** was described as a/an _____ horse
ADJECTIVE

with a pointy _____ in the middle of its _____,
NOUN   PART OF THE BODY

a billy-goat beard, a lion's _____, and _____
NOUN   ADJECTIVE

hooves. It was believed to bring _____ luck to those
ADJECTIVE

who were fortunate enough to see it.

• The **griffin** had the body of a/an _____ and the
NOUN

head and _____ of an eagle. Legend has it that they
PLURAL NOUN

guarded treasures of priceless _____. It is also
PLURAL NOUN

believed they had the power to make a/an _____
ADJECTIVE

man see.

MAD LIBS® is fun to play with friends, but you can also play it by yourself! To begin with, DO NOT look at the story on the page below. Fill in the blanks on this page with the words called for. Then, using the words you have selected, fill in the blank spaces in the story.

Now you've created your own hilarious MAD LIBS® game!

CATS VS. DOGS, PART 1

ADJECTIVE _____

ADJECTIVE _____

VERB _____

NOUN _____

PLURAL NOUN _____

NOUN _____

PART OF THE BODY (PLURAL) _____

NOUN _____

ADJECTIVE _____

PART OF THE BODY _____

ADJECTIVE _____

PART OF THE BODY _____

NUMBER _____

MAD LIBS®

CATS VS. DOGS, PART 1

The _____ debate remains: Which pet is better, a cat or a dog?
_____ADJECTIVE

Here are some *purr*-fect reasons why cats make _____ pets:
_____ADJECTIVE

• Cats come and _____ as they please, exploring the
_____VERB

neighbor's _____, climbing tall _____, or
_____NOUN_____PLURAL NOUN

basking in the midday _____.
_____NOUN

• Cats are mysterious. Take one look into a cat's diamond-shaped

_____, and you're sure it's reading your _____.
PART OF THE BODY (PLURAL)_____NOUN

• Cats are known for their _____ cleanliness. They wash
_____ADJECTIVE

themselves by licking their fur with their scratchy _____.
_____PART OF THE BODY

• Cats purr. It's a truly _____ sound that can even win
_____ADJECTIVE

the _____ of a non-cat lover.
____PART OF THE BODY

• Finally, a cat is reputed to have _____ lives, which
_____NUMBER

makes it the cat's meow!

From MAD ABOUT ANIMALS MAD LIBS® • Copyright © 2009 by Price Stern Sloan,
a division of Penguin Young Readers Group, 345 Hudson Street, New York, NY 10014.

MAD LIBS® is fun to play with friends, but you can also play it by yourself! To begin with, DO NOT look at the story on the page below. Fill in the blanks on this page with the words called for. Then, using the words you have selected, fill in the blank spaces in the story.

Now you've created your own hilarious MAD LIBS® game!

CATS VS. DOGS, PART 2

ADJECTIVE _____

NOUN _____

ADJECTIVE _____

NOUN _____

ADVERB _____

PART OF THE BODY _____

NUMBER _____

NOUN _____

ADJECTIVE _____

ADJECTIVE _____

NUMBER _____

ADJECTIVE _____

ADJECTIVE _____

ADJECTIVE _____

NOUN _____

NOUN _____

NOUN _____

NOUN _____

MAD LIBS®
CATS VS. DOGS, PART 2

Now, from the opposing side—here are a few _____

ADJECTIVE

reasons why dogs are considered man's best _____ :

NOUN

- Dogs are _____ companions. They love to play. You can

ADJECTIVE

  throw a rubber _____ and a dog will _____

NOUN   ADVERB

  chase it and carry it back to you in its _____ at least

PART OF THE BODY

  _____ times.

NUMBER

- Dogs can keep your _____ safe. Their _____

NOUN   ADJECTIVE

  sense of hearing and _____ sense of smell justify the

ADJECTIVE

  term *watchdog*.

- There are more than _____ breeds of dogs. You can

NUMBER

  pick a/an _____ Chihuahua or a/an _____

ADJECTIVE   ADJECTIVE

  Dane, and each will have its own _____ personality.

ADJECTIVE

- You can't get a more loyal _____ than a dog. Just

NOUN

  rub a dog's _____ and you will have a/an _____

NOUN   NOUN

  for life.

- And the good news—a dog's bark is usually worse than its _____ !

NOUN

MAD LIBS® is fun to play with friends, but you can also play it by yourself! To begin with, DO NOT look at the story on the page below. Fill in the blanks on this page with the words called for. Then, using the words you have selected, fill in the blank spaces in the story.

Now you've created your own hilarious MAD LIBS® game!

DINO-MITE

ADJECTIVE _____

VERB (PAST TENSE) _____

PERSON IN ROOM _____

ADJECTIVE _____

PART OF THE BODY _____

PLURAL NOUN_____

NOUN _____

PLURAL NOUN_____

ADJECTIVE _____

ADJECTIVE _____

NOUN _____

ADJECTIVE _____

ADJECTIVE _____

PLURAL NOUN _____

NOUN _____

ADJECTIVE _____

TYPE OF LIQUID _____

PLURAL NOUN_____

PLURAL NOUN_____

NOUN _____

MAD LIBS®
DINO-MITE

Millions of years ago, _____ creatures called dinosaurs
                   ADJECTIVE

_____ all over the earth. The largest was the Tyrannosaurus
VERB (PAST TENSE)

_____. Strangely, this _____ beast had a small
PERSON IN ROOM   ADJECTIVE

_____ and was a scavenger that ate mostly _____.
PART OF THE BODY   PLURAL NOUN

The brontosaurus, an herbivore, had a very long _____,
                                      NOUN

which helped it reach up and eat _____ from the tops of
                          PLURAL NOUN

_____ trees. The stegosaurus had _____ scales that
ADJECTIVE   ADJECTIVE

were used as armor when it was attacked by a/an _____,
                                NOUN

and it ate a variety of _____ fruits and _____
                   ADJECTIVE   ADJECTIVE

foliage. Unfortunately, dinosaurs disappeared long before human

_____ appeared on earth. What happened to them?
PLURAL NOUN

Scientists think a giant _____ fell from space, creating a/an
                        NOUN

_____ wave of _____ and dust that destroyed these
ADJECTIVE   TYPE OF LIQUID

magnificent _____. Today, archeologists are still digging up
              PLURAL NOUN

dinosaur _____, which can be seen in museums all over the
          PLURAL NOUN

_____.
NOUN

From MAD ABOUT ANIMALS MAD LIBS® • Copyright © 2009 by Price Stern Sloan,
a division of Penguin Young Readers Group, 345 Hudson Street, New York, NY 10014.

MAD LIBS® is fun to play with friends, but you can also play it by yourself! To begin with, DO NOT look at the story on the page below. Fill in the blanks on this page with the words called for. Then, using the words you have selected, fill in the blank spaces in the story.

Now you've created your own hilarious MAD LIBS® game!

AMAZING DADS

ADJECTIVE _____

PLURAL NOUN _____

PLURAL NOUN _____

ADJECTIVE _____

ADJECTIVE _____

NUMBER _____

ADJECTIVE _____

PLURAL NOUN _____

NOUN _____

PART OF THE BODY _____

ADJECTIVE _____

PLURAL NOUN _____

NOUN _____

ADJECTIVE _____

ADJECTIVE _____

PART OF THE BODY _____

NUMBER _____

ADJECTIVE _____

NOUN _____

You hear a lot about _____ mothers in the wild,
ADJECTIVE

nurturing and taking care of their _____. But what most
PLURAL NOUN

_____ don't know is that there are a lot of great animal
PLURAL NOUN

dads, too. A/An _____ example is the _____
ADJECTIVE   ADJECTIVE

sea horse. After a courtship dance of _____ hours, the
NUMBER

female gives her _____ eggs to the male, who carries them
ADJECTIVE

until they hatch. Emperor penguins are hands-on _____, too.
PLURAL NOUN

After the mother lays a/an _____, the dad carries it in his
NOUN

_____ to keep it _____ and warm while
PART OF THE BODY   ADJECTIVE

she goes off to look for _____ to eat. He holds on to the
PLURAL NOUN

_____ throughout the cold, _____ winter.
NOUN   ADJECTIVE

Another example of dad care is the _____ cardinal fish.
ADJECTIVE

After the female fertilizes the eggs, the proud father keeps them in

his _____ for _____ days, until they hatch.
PART OF THE BODY   NUMBER

Each of these _____ fathers deserves a trophy that says
ADJECTIVE

"World's #1 _____!"
NOUN

From MAD ABOUT ANIMALS MAD LIBS® • Copyright © 2009 by Price Stern Sloan,
a division of Penguin Young Readers Group, 345 Hudson Street, New York, NY 10014.

MAD LIBS® is fun to play with friends, but you can also play it by yourself! To begin with, DO NOT look at the story on the page below. Fill in the blanks on this page with the words called for. Then, using the words you have selected, fill in the blank spaces in the story.

Now you've created your own hilarious MAD LIBS® game!

PANDAMANIA

PLURAL NOUN _____

ADJECTIVE _____

NOUN _____

ADJECTIVE _____

NOUN _____

VERB ENDING IN "ING" _____

PLURAL NOUN _____

EXCLAMATION _____

PART OF THE BODY (PLURAL) _____

ADJECTIVE _____

PART OF THE BODY (PLURAL) _____

NOUN _____

NOUN _____

NOUN _____

PLURAL NOUN _____

PLURAL NOUN _____

MAD LIBS®
PANDAMANIA

Welcome back to the *World of Wild* _____. When we
                                        PLURAL NOUN

left off, we were tracking the _____ panda in the forests
                                        ADJECTIVE

of China, hoping to catch a glimpse of a newborn _____.
                                                            NOUN

Now, we are making our way through the _____
                                                    ADJECTIVE

bamboo forest, trying to be as quiet as a/an _____.
                                                        NOUN

Wait! Something is _____ behind a bush! We can't
                        VERB ENDING IN "ING"

see it, so we have to part some thick bamboo _____.
                                                        PLURAL NOUN

_____! I can't believe my _____. There
        EXCLAMATION   PART OF THE BODY (PLURAL)

is a mother panda, cradling her _____ cub in her
                                            ADJECTIVE

_____. The baby is the size of a miniature
PART OF THE BODY (PLURAL)

_____! It's the most beautiful _____
        NOUN   NOUN

I've ever seen. Uh-oh, the mother _____ doesn't
                                            NOUN

look too happy that we're here. Oh my _____, it
                                                PLURAL NOUN

looks like she's coming after us! Run for your _____!
                                                        PLURAL NOUN

MAD LIBS® is fun to play with friends, but you can also play it by yourself! To begin with, DO NOT look at the story on the page below. Fill in the blanks on this page with the words called for. Then, using the words you have selected, fill in the blank spaces in the story.

Now you've created your own hilarious MAD LIBS® game!

DOLPHINSPEAK

ADJECTIVE _____

PLURAL NOUN _____

NOUN _____

ADJECTIVE _____

PLURAL NOUN _____

ADJECTIVE _____

ADJECTIVE _____

PLURAL NOUN _____

ADJECTIVE _____

PLURAL NOUN _____

PART OF THE BODY (PLURAL) _____

OCCUPATION _____

ADJECTIVE _____

PERSON IN ROOM _____

ADVERB _____

MAD LIBS®
DOLPHINSPEAK

Humans have many _____ ways of communicating with
            ADJECTIVE

one another. Today we depend on TV, cell _____, and
                                        PLURAL NOUN

e-_____ to get our information. Dolphins may not use
        NOUN

technology as _____ as ours, but they are highly
                ADJECTIVE

advanced _____ with a/an _____ capacity
            PLURAL NOUN   ADJECTIVE

for language skills. They communicate by making _____
                                                    ADJECTIVE

noises that sound like _____, called sonar. Their
                            PLURAL NOUN

_____ sounds bounce off underwater _____,
    ADJECTIVE   PLURAL NOUN

traveling to the _____ of other dolphins. This
                PART OF THE BODY (PLURAL)

makes it easy for dolphins to alert their friends that there's a

deep-sea _____ swimming nearby, or to share the
            OCCUPATION

latest _____ gossip about _____. So the
        ADJECTIVE   PERSON IN ROOM

next time you're at an aquarium, listen _____
                                            ADVERB

to the dolphins: They might just be talking about you!

MAD LIBS® is fun to play with friends, but you can also play it by yourself! To begin with, DO NOT look at the story on the page below. Fill in the blanks on this page with the words called for. Then, using the words you have selected, fill in the blank spaces in the story.

Now you've created your own hilarious MAD LIBS® game!

IN THE NURSERY, PART 1

ADJECTIVE _____

ADJECTIVE _____

ADJECTIVE _____

ADJECTIVE _____

PLURAL NOUN _____

VERB ENDING IN "ING" _____

ADJECTIVE _____

PLURAL NOUN _____

NOUN _____

NUMBER _____

ADJECTIVE _____

NOUN _____

PLURAL NOUN _____

PLURAL NOUN _____

PLURAL NOUN _____

ADVERB _____

ADJECTIVE _____

NOUN _____

NOUN _____

IN THE NURSERY, PART 1

Most _____ bedtime stories revolve around _____
ADJECTIVE   ADJECTIVE

animals—and they usually end happily. Here are some _____
ADJECTIVE

examples of this theory:

• "The Three _____ Pigs": The pigs build houses made
ADJECTIVE

of straw, sticks, and _____. By huffing and _____,
PLURAL NOUN   VERB ENDING IN "ING"

the big, _____ wolf blows the first two _____
ADJECTIVE   PLURAL NOUN

down—but he just can't blow down the brick _____.
NOUN

• "Goldilocks and the _____ Bears": While the _____
NUMBER   ADJECTIVE

bears are away, Goldilocks sneaks in their house, eats their

_____, sits in their _____, and sleeps in
NOUN   PLURAL NOUN

their _____. The three _____ come home,
PLURAL NOUN   PLURAL NOUN

but Goldilocks _____ escapes.
ADVERB

• "The Frog Prince": A/An _____ princess befriends
ADJECTIVE

a frog, but when she kisses his _____, he transforms
NOUN

into a handsome _____.
NOUN

MAD LIBS® is fun to play with friends, but you can also play it by yourself! To begin with, DO NOT look at the story on the page below. Fill in the blanks on this page with the words called for. Then, using the words you have selected, fill in the blank spaces in the story.

Now you've created your own hilarious MAD LIBS® game!

IN THE NURSERY, PART 2

NOUN _____

NOUN _____

PLURAL NOUN _____

VERB _____

ADJECTIVE _____

NOUN _____

ADJECTIVE _____

ADJECTIVE _____

ADJECTIVE _____

ADJECTIVE _____

PART OF THE BODY (PLURAL) _____

PLURAL NOUN _____

ADJECTIVE _____

PLURAL NOUN _____

NOUN _____

PLURAL NOUN _____

ADJECTIVE _____

ADJECTIVE _____

MAD LIBS®

IN THE NURSERY, PART 2

- "Little Red Riding _____": This story features another
  _____ NOUN

  big, bad _____. This wolf disguises himself as Little
  _____ NOUN

  Red's grandmother. "My, what big _____ you have!" she
  _____ PLURAL NOUN

  cries. "The better to _____ you with, my dear," the wolf
  _____ VERB

  replies. Ultimately, Little Red _____ Hood is rescued by
  _____ ADJECTIVE

  a/an _____.
  _____ NOUN

- "The _____ Duckling": The duckling feels he's
  _____ ADJECTIVE

  more _____ than the other ducks. All his friends taunt
  _____ ADJECTIVE

  him: "Look how _____ he is! He's not one of us!"
  _____ ADJECTIVE

  When he turns into a/an _____ swan, they can't believe
  _____ ADJECTIVE

  their _____.
  _____ PART OF THE BODY (PLURAL)

- "Puss in _____": A/An _____ miller's son
  _____ PLURAL NOUN _____ ADJECTIVE

  inherits a cat who promises him riches and _____ in
  _____ PLURAL NOUN

  return for a bag containing a/an _____ and a pair
  _____ NOUN

  of high leather _____. Eventually the _____
  _____ PLURAL NOUN _____ ADJECTIVE

  son marries a/an _____ princess.
  _____ ADJECTIVE

MAD LIBS® is fun to play with friends, but you can also play it by yourself! To begin with, DO NOT look at the story on the page below. Fill in the blanks on this page with the words called for. Then, using the words you have selected, fill in the blank spaces in the story.

Now you've created your own hilarious MAD LIBS® game!

FIRST PETS

COLOR _____

ADJECTIVE _____

NOUN _____

ADJECTIVE _____

NOUN _____

PLURAL NOUN _____

NOUN _____

NOUN _____

SILLY WORD _____

PERSON IN ROOM _____

ADJECTIVE _____

PERSON IN ROOM _____

PERSON IN ROOM _____

ADJECTIVE _____

NOUN _____

ADJECTIVE _____

VERB _____

ADJECTIVE _____

MAD LIBS®

FIRST PETS

When an American president gets elected, the entire family moves

into the _____ House—including their _____

COLOR · ADJECTIVE

pets. Our first _____, George Washington, had seven

NOUN

_____ hounds, horses, and even a parrot that said, "Polly

ADJECTIVE

want a/an _____." John Quincy Adams owned silkworms

NOUN

that made _____ for his wife. Zachary Taylor kept a horse

PLURAL NOUN

on the front lawn of the White _____. Calvin Coolidge

NOUN

owned enough animals for a zoo, including a pygmy_____,

NOUN

a pair of birds named _____ and _____, and

SILLY WORD · PERSON IN ROOM

even a/an _____ wallaby. John F. Kennedy had two

ADJECTIVE

hamsters named _____ and _____. More recently,

PERSON IN ROOM · PERSON IN ROOM

President Clinton had a/an _____ cat named Socks, who

ADJECTIVE

didn't get along with their Labrador _____ named

NOUN

Buddy. So now you know how_____ politicians learned

ADJECTIVE

to _____ like cats and dogs—from their _____ pets!

VERB · ADJECTIVE

From MAD ABOUT ANIMALS MAD LIBS® • Copyright © 2009 by Price Stern Sloan,
a division of Penguin Young Readers Group, 345 Hudson Street, New York, NY 10014.

MAD LIBS® is fun to play with friends, but you can also play it by yourself! To begin with, DO NOT look at the story on the page below. Fill in the blanks on this page with the words called for. Then, using the words you have selected, fill in the blank spaces in the story.

Now you've created your own hilarious MAD LIBS® game!

THE KING OF BUTTERFLIES

PLURAL NOUN _____

ADJECTIVE _____

NOUN _____

ADJECTIVE _____

ADJECTIVE _____

NUMBER _____

ADJECTIVE _____

PLURAL NOUN _____

PLURAL NOUN _____

ADJECTIVE _____

ADJECTIVE _____

PLURAL NOUN _____

ADJECTIVE _____

PART OF THE BODY (PLURAL) _____

MAD LIBS®

THE KING OF BUTTERFLIES

The monarch butterfly, with its distinctive black and yellow

_____, is one of the most _____ insects on
PLURAL NOUN   ADJECTIVE

the planet. But it doesn't start life as a beautiful _____.
                                                                          NOUN

A monarch egg first hatches into a/an _____ caterpillar
                                                       ADJECTIVE

that spins a/an _____ covering made of silk called a
                          ADJECTIVE

cocoon. Over a period of _____ weeks, the caterpillar
                                          NUMBER

turns into a/an _____ butterfly. When the monarch
                          ADJECTIVE

is able to spread its _____, it flies away to feed on a
                                      PLURAL NOUN

variety of _____, including milkweed, red clover, and
                      PLURAL NOUN

other _____ flowers. Monarchs are especially noted
                ADJECTIVE

for their _____ migrations across the country and,
                      ADJECTIVE

upon occasion, across the Atlantic and Pacific _____.
                                                                          PLURAL NOUN

In flight, these _____ butterflies are a sight for sore
                            ADJECTIVE

_____!
PART OF THE BODY (PLURAL)

From MAD ABOUT ANIMALS MAD LIBS® • Copyright © 2009 by Price Stern Sloan,
a division of Penguin Young Readers Group, 345 Hudson Street, New York, NY 10014.

MAD LIBS® is fun to play with friends, but you can also play it by yourself! To begin with, DO NOT look at the story on the page below. Fill in the blanks on this page with the words called for. Then, using the words you have selected, fill in the blank spaces in the story.

Now you've created your own hilarious MAD LIBS® game!

SNAKE SCARE

PLURAL NOUN _____

SILLY WORD _____

PLURAL NOUN _____

ADJECTIVE _____

PART OF THE BODY _____

VERB ENDING IN "ING" _____

ADJECTIVE _____

ADJECTIVE _____

NOUN _____

PART OF THE BODY _____

VERB (PAST TENSE) _____

NOUN _____

PART OF THE BODY (PLURAL) _____

ADJECTIVE _____

NOUN _____

NOUN _____

PART OF THE BODY _____

VERB _____

MAD☺LIBS®

SNAKE SCARE

In my opinion, snakes are the scariest _____ on the planet.
PLURAL NOUN

My fear of snakes began when I was away at Camp _____
SILLY WORD

one summer. We were seated around a campfire roasting

_____ on sticks when I became very tired and decided
PLURAL NOUN

to go back to my _____ cabin to catch some shut-
ADJECTIVE

_____. I was snug in my _____ bag when
PART OF THE BODY   VERB ENDING IN "ING"

I suddenly felt something _____ touching my leg. At first
ADJECTIVE

I thought it was a/an _____ dream, but then I heard a
ADJECTIVE

hissing like a boiling tea _____, and felt something
NOUN

slithering up my _____! I _____ at the top of
PART OF THE BODY   VERB (PAST TENSE)

my lungs and was out of my _____ in a split second. I ran
NOUN

as fast as my _____ could carry me and dove into
PART OF THE BODY (PLURAL)

the _____ pond, hoping to ditch the snake. To my
ADJECTIVE

embarrassment, it turned out to be a harmless garter _____.
NOUN

But today, just the thought of a snake's scaly _____ and
NOUN

rattling _____ makes my skin _____!
PART OF THE BODY   VERB

From MAD ABOUT ANIMALS MAD LIBS® • Copyright © 2009 by Price Stern Sloan,
a division of Penguin Young Readers Group, 345 Hudson Street, New York, NY 10014.

MAD LIBS® is fun to play with friends, but you can also play it by yourself! To begin with, DO NOT look at the story on the page below. Fill in the blanks on this page with the words called for. Then, using the words you have selected, fill in the blank spaces in the story.

Now you've created your own hilarious MAD LIBS® game!

FELINE PHARAOHS

ADJECTIVE _____

ADJECTIVE _____

PLURAL NOUN _____

ADJECTIVE _____

NOUN _____

PLURAL NOUN _____

ADJECTIVE _____

NOUN _____

VERB ENDING IN "ING" _____

ADJECTIVE _____

PART OF THE BODY _____

PLURAL NOUN _____

ADJECTIVE _____

ADJECTIVE _____

NOUN _____

PLURAL NOUN _____

NOUN _____

MAD LIBS®

FELINE PHARAOHS

In the ancient land of _____ mummies and _____
                              ADJECTIVE   ADJECTIVE

pyramids, it was great to be a cat. All of today's cats are descended

from those ancient _____ of Egypt. Beginning as a wild
                           PLURAL NOUN

and _____ species, the cat was quickly domesticated
        ADJECTIVE

and became a symbol of grace and _____. Kings, queens,
                                              NOUN

and even common _____ discovered that cats made
                        PLURAL NOUN

_____ companions. Before long, felines became revered
   ADJECTIVE

in Egyptian society. Every Egyptian _____ believed
                                              NOUN

that if you saw a cat while you were _____ seeds, you
                                         VERB ENDING IN "ING"

would have a/an _____ harvest. Images of cats were
                     ADJECTIVE

seen on everything from jewelry for the _____ to
                                              PART OF THE BODY

cat-shaped _____ that women wore in their _____
               PLURAL NOUN   ADJECTIVE

hair. Many homes had _____ 14-karat _____
                          ADJECTIVE   NOUN

cat statues. Egyptians even mummified cats, so that their owners

could spend the afterlife with their beloved _____!
                                                  PLURAL NOUN

Isn't that the _____'s meow?
                    NOUN

MAD LIBS® is fun to play with friends, but you can also play it by yourself! To begin with, DO NOT look at the story on the page below. Fill in the blanks on this page with the words called for. Then, using the words you have selected, fill in the blank spaces in the story.

Now you've created your own hilarious MAD LIBS® game!

DOWN ON THE FARM

PERSON IN ROOM (FEMALE) _____

ADJECTIVE _____

VERB ENDING IN "ING" _____

NOUN _____

PLURAL NOUN _____

NOUN _____

ADJECTIVE _____

PLURAL NOUN _____

PLURAL NOUN _____

ADJECTIVE _____

ADJECTIVE _____

PLURAL NOUN _____

PERSON IN ROOM _____

ADJECTIVE _____

PART OF THE BODY _____

NOUN _____

ADJECTIVE _____

MAD LIBS®

DOWN ON THE FARM

My summer vacation on Aunt _____'s farm
PERSON IN ROOM (FEMALE)

has been fun, but it's also been a lot of _____ work.
ADJECTIVE

This morning, as usual, I woke up as the rooster was

_____, and ate a hearty _____ of
VERB ENDING IN "ING"   NOUN

_____ and syrup, with eggs freshly laid by the
PLURAL NOUN

farm _____. Then, I went out to the _____
NOUN   ADJECTIVE

barn to do my chores. I fed and groomed the horses, brushing

their _____ and cleaning their _____.
PLURAL NOUN   PLURAL NOUN

I also cleaned their _____ trough, which smelled
ADJECTIVE

like _____ _____. Finally, I milked
ADJECTIVE   PLURAL NOUN

_____, the cow. I sat on a/an _____
PERSON IN ROOM   ADJECTIVE

stool beneath the cow's _____, and filled an
PART OF THE BODY

entire _____ full of fresh milk. Yup, just another
NOUN

_____ day down on the farm!
ADJECTIVE

From MAD ABOUT ANIMALS MAD LIBS® • Copyright © 2009 by Price Stern Sloan,
a division of Penguin Young Readers Group, 345 Hudson Street, New York, NY 10014.

MAD LIBS® is fun to play with friends, but you can also play it by yourself! To begin with, DO NOT look at the story on the page below. Fill in the blanks on this page with the words called for. Then, using the words you have selected, fill in the blank spaces in the story.

Now you've created your own hilarious MAD LIBS® game!

QUEEN BEE

PLURAL NOUN _____

ADJECTIVE _____

NOUN _____

VERB _____

ADJECTIVE _____

ADJECTIVE _____

NOUN _____

ADJECTIVE _____

ADJECTIVE _____

PLURAL NOUN _____

TYPE OF LIQUID _____

PLURAL NOUN _____

NOUN _____

PLURAL NOUN _____

ADJECTIVE _____

ADJECTIVE _____

MAD LIBS®

QUEEN BEE

The following is an interview with a Bee Bee C bee reporter and a

Queen Bee, to be read aloud by two _____ .

PLURAL NOUN

Q: We are here with Her _____ Highness, the Queen

ADJECTIVE

_____ , who has agreed to _____ with

NOUN　　　　　　　　　　　　　　　　　VERB

us today. Your Highness, describe your _____ hive.

ADJECTIVE

A: I am proud to reign over forty thousand _____ bees

ADJECTIVE

who work around the _____ . You know what they

NOUN

say, "As _____ as a bee!"

ADJECTIVE

Q: What are some _____ bee facts that we may not know?

ADJECTIVE

A: Well, I lay over two thousand _____ a day. Other

PLURAL NOUN

bees do everything from making sweet golden _____

TYPE OF LIQUID

to pollinating _____ . And each bee has its own

PLURAL NOUN

unique _____ so that I can tell them apart.

NOUN

Q: Any other _____ of wisdom for this _____

PLURAL NOUN　　　　　　　　　　　　　　　ADJECTIVE

reporter?

A: Honey, _____ words may sting you, but just *bee* yourself.

ADJECTIVE

This book is published by

PRICE STERN SLOAN

whose other splendid titles include
such literary classics as